Water is Life Different Sources of Water and Ways to Conserve Them

(For Early Science Learners)

Speedy Publishing LLC
40 E. Main St. #1156
Newark, DE 19711
www.speedypublishing.com

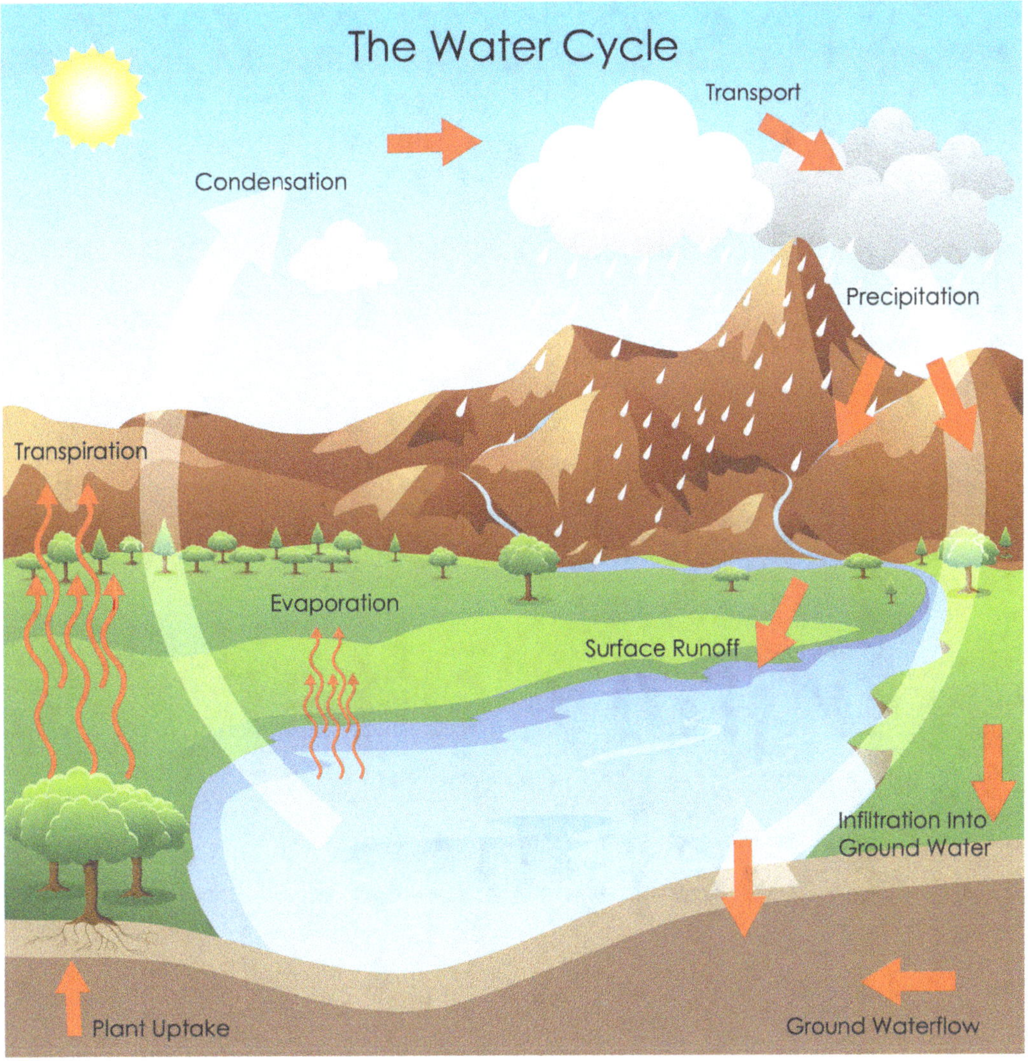

The Water Cycle

Transport

Condensation

Precipitation

Transpiration

Evaporation

Surface Runoff

Infiltration Into Ground Water

Plant Uptake

Ground Waterflow

TIPS ON CONSERVING WATER

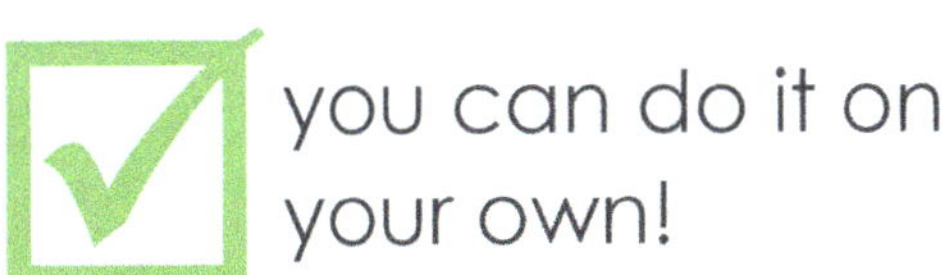

you can do it on your own!

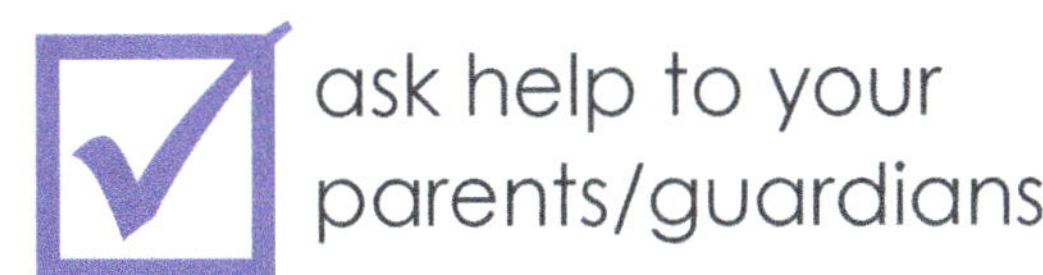

ask help to your parents/guardians

 **Turn off faucets tightly after each use.**

 **Check faucets and pipes for leaks.**

 **Take shorter showers.**

 **Turn off the water after you wet your toothbrush.**

 **When washing dishes by hand, don't leave the water running for rinsing.**

 **Keep a bottle of drinking water in the fridge.**

 **Wash your fruits and vegetables in a pan of water instead of running water from the tap.**

save

 **Learn how to use your water meter to check for leaks.**

 **Collect the water you use while rinsing fruit and vegetables. Use it to water house plants.**

If you accidentally drop ice cubes, don't throw them in the sink. Drop them in a house plant instead.

 **Cook food in as little water as possible. This also helps it retain more nutrients.**

 **Toilet leaks can be silent! Be sure to test your toilet for leaks at least once a year.**

 **When washing your hands, turn the water off while you lather.**

 **Use water you collected from washing dishes to wash your car.**